Andrew Langley

MONSTER MACHINES

Illustrated by
Mike Atkinson

Language Consultant:
Diana Bentley
University of Reading

PUFFIN BOOKS

Words printed in
bold are explained
in the glossary

Contents

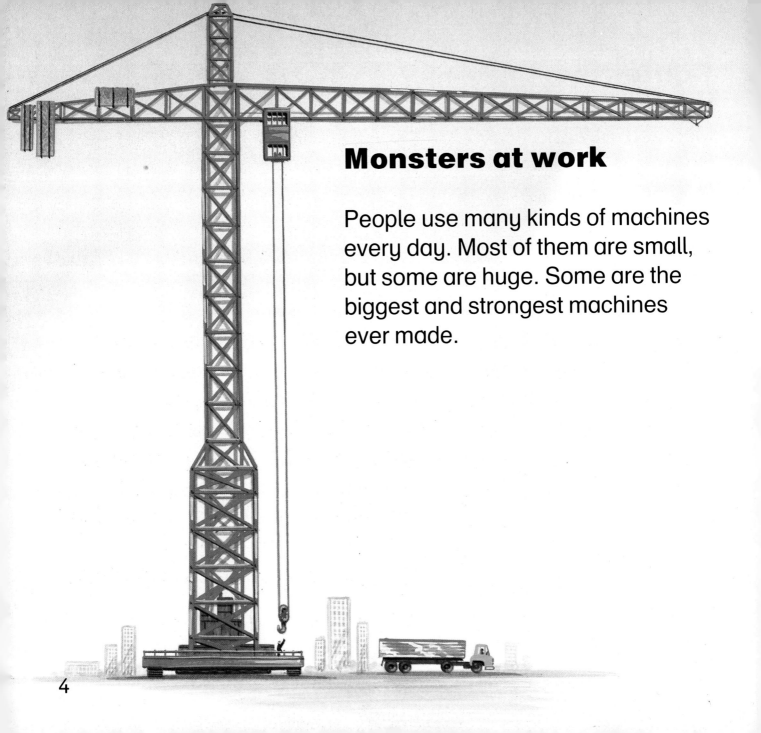

Monsters at work

People use many kinds of machines every day. Most of them are small, but some are huge. Some are the biggest and strongest machines ever made.

These monster machines do many different jobs. Huge trucks, ships and aircraft carry goods around the world. Diggers move earth and rocks. Cutting machines dig out mines and tunnels. Tall windmills use the power of the wind to make electricity. Massive harvesters cut the crops in the fields.

6

Cargo carriers

Giant trucks carry heavy loads over long distances. They are made in two parts. At the front is the tractor, with the powerful engine and the cab for the driver. At the back is the trailer, where the load is stored.

The biggest trucks of all are the road trains in Australia and the USA. These pull two or three huge trailers. They travel on straight dirt roads across wide open spaces. A road train takes a long time to stop. The driver blows a loud horn to warn people to get out of the way.

Monsters for space

Scientists need monster machines to help them explore outer space.

The *Crawler* is the huge moving platform which carries the **space shuttle** to its launch pad at Cape Canaveral in the USA. The *Crawler* is the largest transporter in the world. It has eight sets of **caterpillar tracks**. Its top speed is only 3 km per hour.

The space shuttle is launched on the back of a huge rocket. The rocket is needed to thrust the space shuttle out of the Earth's **atmosphere.**

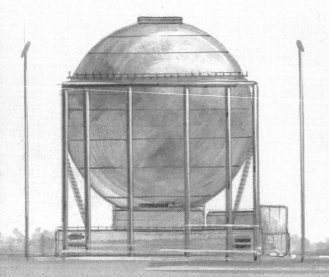

Giants at sea

Oil tankers are by far the world's biggest ships. They transport **crude oil** from the Middle East to Europe, the USA and Canada. Some tankers are long enough to hold five football pitches! They are so heavy that they take more than 6 km to stop.

The USS *Nimitz* is a giant aircraft carrier. It has a crew of 6,300 people, and can carry more than 90 aircraft beneath its decks. The *Nimitz* is driven by **nuclear power**.

Trenching machine

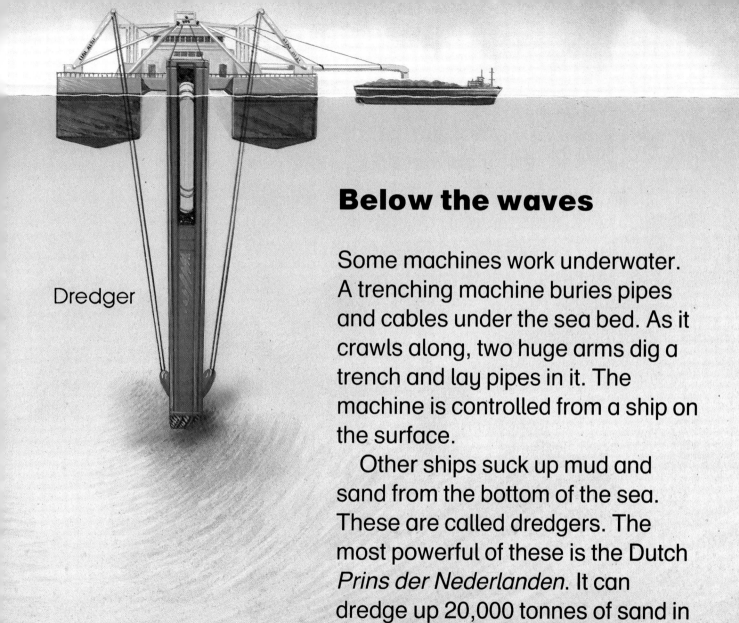

Dredger

Below the waves

Some machines work underwater. A trenching machine buries pipes and cables under the sea bed. As it crawls along, two huge arms dig a trench and lay pipes in it. The machine is controlled from a ship on the surface.

Other ships suck up mud and sand from the bottom of the sea. These are called dredgers. The most powerful of these is the Dutch *Prins der Nederlanden*. It can dredge up 20,000 tonnes of sand in less than one hour.

13

Monsters on rails

The first railway **locomotives** were driven by **steam engines**. One of the biggest steam locomotives was *Big Boy*, which was built in the USA in 1941. *Big Boy* had 24 wheels, and was made of several sections joined together so that it could go round bends in the track.

Locomotives today are nearly all powered by electric or **diesel engines**. The strongest ones are the locomotives used by the Union Pacific Railway in the USA. Two or more of these are joined together to pull trains which are several kilometres long.

Giants of the skies

Jumbo jets are huge airliners. They are called jumbos because of their giant size. A jumbo can fly across the Atlantic Ocean with more than 400 passengers on board.

The biggest aircraft ever built was a **flying boat** called *Spruce Goose*. It was built in the USA and had a wing span of 97 m. This is about as long as a football pitch! *Spruce Goose* made its one and only flight in 1947.

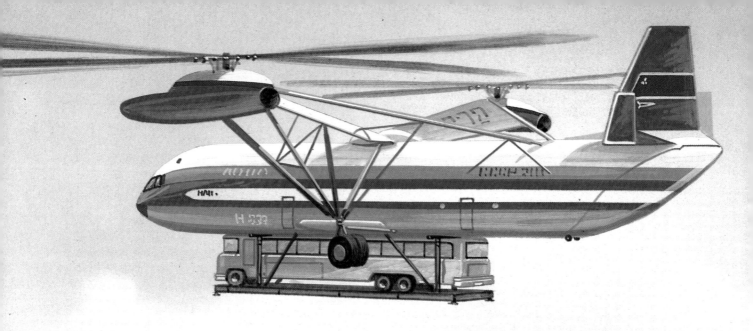

Flying monsters

The world's largest helicopter can pick up enormous loads – even a bus! It is called the *Mi-12 Homer* and it is built in the USSR. The two sets of **rotor blades** are mounted on arms on either side of the body. This helps the helicopter lift very heavy objects.

The US *Galaxy* aircraft can carry a whole army into battle. Its top deck has seats for 100 troops. Below, there is space for tanks and equipment. The *Galaxy's* nose cone opens upwards so that vehicles can be driven inside.

Earth movers

Diggers like this one are used to move earth.

Big Muskie is the largest digger. It is used to dig open coal mines in the USA. Its bucket is so huge that more than one thousand people could stand inside it!

Once the earth has been dug up, it must be moved. This is the job of a dump truck such as the enormous *Titan*. The *Titan* is too big to travel on ordinary roads. It is transported to the site in pieces, and then put together.

21

Under the earth

This machine is called a **tunnel mole**. It digs tunnels under the ground for railways and roads. The cutting head at the front moves forward into the rock at about 2 m per hour. The rubble is carried away by **conveyor belts** and the tunnel is lined with concrete or steel.

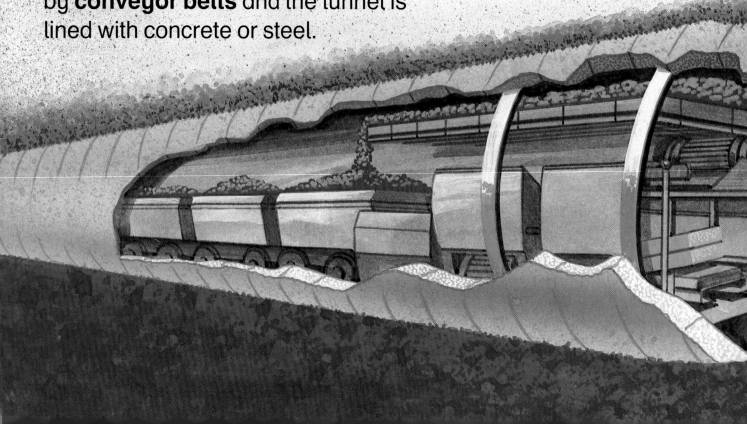

A special kind of cutter is used in coal mining. It passes along the coal face and its steel cutters tear out the coal. Water is sprayed on the cutting head to keep it cool.

Cranes and lifters

Cranes are used for lifting and moving heavy objects. Some load and unload ships. Others are used on building sites to lift steel **girders** and other materials.

The biggest moving crane in the world is called *Rosenkranz*. This crane is so large that it has to be carried on ten trucks.

A fork-lift truck can also pick up heavy loads. It lifts them on two metal prongs. Giant fork-lifts can lift loads as big as 80 tonnes.

On the farm

Many farmers today grow their crops in huge fields. They use monster machines to sow seeds and harvest the corn.

The seeds are sown by seed drills pulled by huge tractors. These machines plant seeds in the ground through thin pipes.

The crops are cut by a giant machine called a combine harvester. The combine separates the straw from the grain. The straw is packed into bales. The grain is sent through a pipe into a lorry.

Monster power

Huge machines are now being built to make electricity in new ways. Giant windmills use the energy of the wind to make power. At one 'wind farm' in the USA there are 86 mills. They produce enough electricity to power a town.

In the future, we may also take energy from an **ocean current** called the Gulf Stream. A huge wheel will be built on the bottom of the ocean. The current will turn the wheel, which will generate electricity.

Glossary

Atmosphere   The air around the Earth.

Caterpillar tracks   Loops of metal treads stretched around the wheels of a vehicle. Caterpillar tracks help large vehicles move over rough ground.

Conveyor belt   A moving strip of metal or material used for transporting objects.

Crude oil   Oil which has not been purified.

Diesel engine   An engine which uses diesel oil for fuel. Most heavy vehicles have diesel engines.

Flying boat   An aircraft which can take off and land on water. Flying boats have floats on their wings instead of wheels.

Girders   Steel beams used as supports in modern buildings.

Locomotive   The engine which pulls a train.

Nuclear power   The energy produced by splitting the nucleus (central part) of an atom.

Ocean current   A steady flow of sea water which always runs in the same direction.

Rotor blades   The metal blades on a helicopter that spin round and lift it off the ground.

Space shuttle   A kind of spacecraft that is able to go into space and then come back to land on Earth again.

Steam engine   An engine which is driven by the power of steam under pressure.

Tunnel mole   A machine which digs tunnels underground. A mole is an animal which lives underground.

Books to read

The Amazing World of Machines, Neil Ardley (Angus & Robertson, 1977)
Biggest Machines, Denise Kiley (Blackwell, 1980)
Machines, Robert O'Brien (Time-Life, 1980)
The Way It Works, Robin Kerrod (Octopus, 1980)

Index